SONGS

of *Joy* in

the Valley of

TEARS

ISBN: 978-1-7364922-0-8

Cover design and interior formatting by Nelly Murariu at PixBeeDesign.com

SONGS
of *Joy* in
the Valley of
TEARS

*A Poetic Journey
through Grief*

JANE AULT

To my twin—

Jean Mildred

(July 25, 1938-June 11, 2020)

PREFACE

My twin sister died on June 11, 2020. Although we lived 1000+ miles from one another for most of our adult lives, our love bond remained strong. We were of kindred spirit. During the spring of the year I knew her health was rapidly declining and had planned to visit her. Because of Covid-19 restrictions, I was neither able to make that trip nor attend her small funeral. It seemed unreal.

Some of the poems I wrote during that time are included in this book. Others are not. The songs and poems I've chosen reflect elements of grief everyone experiences in relationship losses, as well as other losses. They are expressions of my heart written over a period of 37 years.

Songs of Joy in the Valley of Tears is not primarily about physical death. It's about the longing we all have for purpose and meaningful connection within safe, loving relationships. It's about the struggle to find that connection and the faith and energy it takes to remain there.

As you read my book, you will

- ꙮ Connect in healing ways with your losses
- ꙮ Name and process grief in your unique way
- ꙮ Overcome obstacles that block your path
- ꙮ Discover an oasis of hope, peace, and joy in the midst of your tear-filled valley

Through a twin-bond, God gave me an experiential understanding of what it meant to be united in love, having the same mind and being united in spirit, as expressed in Scripture (Philippians 2:2).

It did not always mean agreement of thought but always meant respectful and unconditional acceptance flowing from love. It was an intimate connection of spirit with spirit.

My sister Jean grasped Jesus's love for her earlier in life than I did. She told me about it. I struggled to believe it, to accept love, to find purpose.

My journey through dark valleys reflects not only my sadness about her passing but also the myriads of emotions I've felt over the years in my search to connect more deeply with Jesus and with love.

I've included Scriptures with each poem because they are my source of inspiration. I've meditated on them through the years. As I read them, Jesus speaks to me and meets me in the place where I am. In amazing ways, he clears up my confusion, comforts me, renews my strength, and gives me songs of joy.

CONTENTS

Even if I walk through a very dark valley,
I will not be afraid,
because you are with me.

—Psalm 23:4 (NCV)

Jesus—

**"The path to joy is through
the valley of tears."**

Me—

"Isn't there another way?"

Jesus—

"Follow me. I am the Way."

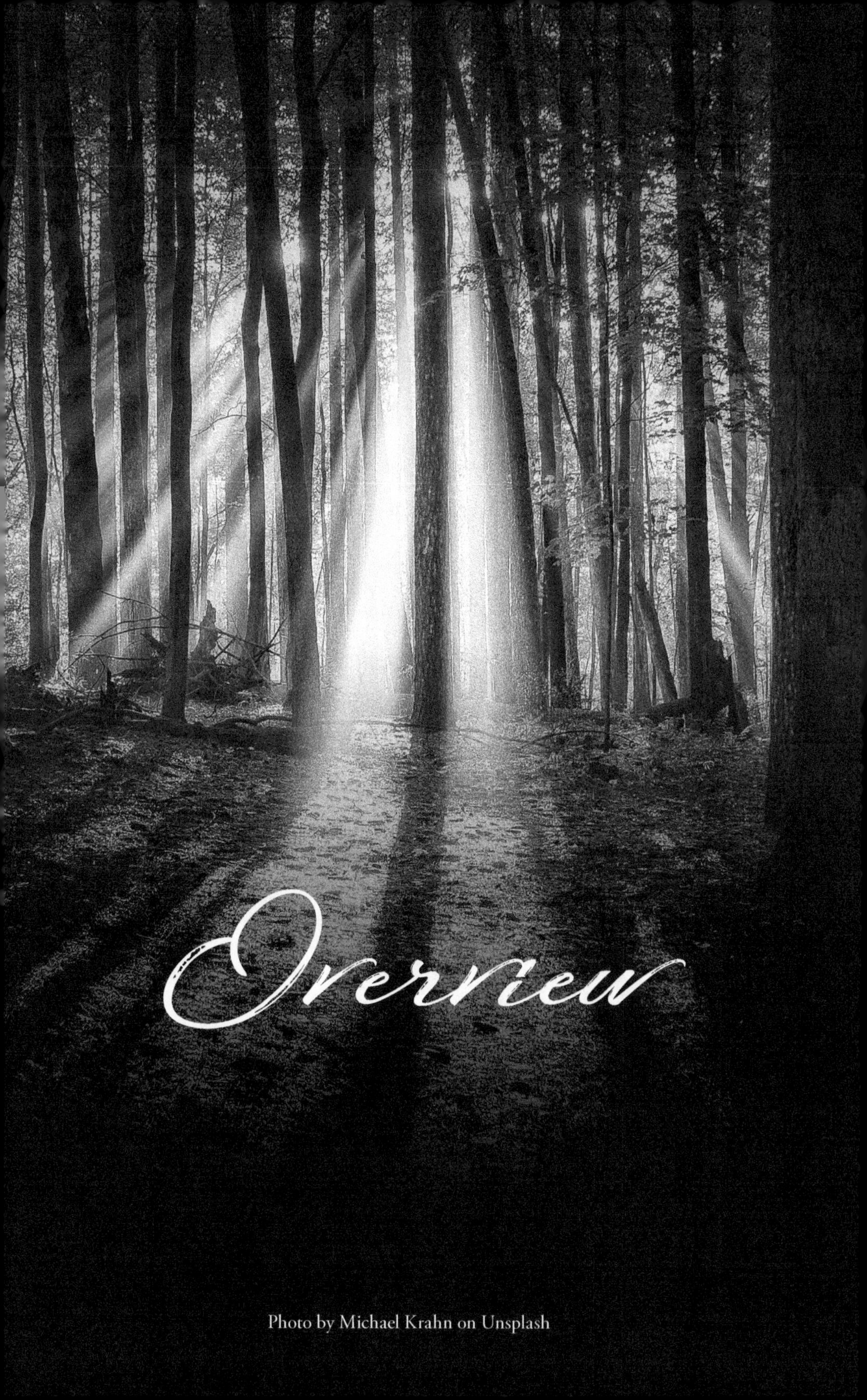

Overview

Photo by Michael Krahn on Unsplash

God's Spirit touches our spirits and confirms who we really are.
We know who he is, and we know who we are: Father and children. And we know we are going to get what's coming to us—an unbelievable inheritance!

—Romans 8:16-18 (MSG)

SONGS

My heart singing to Jesus—
In verse, song, or in silence;
Authentic, unedited, sometimes groaning;

Not always happy and glad,
Sometimes angry, sad, and confused;
Reality, as I understand it,

Not completely accurate,
Because God sees it all and knows what I hide;
His wisdom is far beyond mine.

Jesus's heart singing to me—
Through Scripture, friends, nature,
All of Creation, as I silently listen;

Always in love, always with patience,
Correcting my vision, gracious, forgiving,
Showing me he is far bigger,

Far grander than my small imagination;
He calls me to worship, to trust him further.
I respond with a new melody.

We saw it, we heard it, and now we're telling you so you can experience it along with us, this experience of communion with the Father and his Son, Jesus Christ. Our motive for writing is simply this: We want you to enjoy this, too. Your joy will double our joy!

—1 John 1:3, 4 (MSG)

JOY

Jesus *loves* me.
His "I will never leave you" promise,
"I'm-happy-to-be-with-you" smile, and
  "You bring me delight" eyes tell me it's true.

Jesus is *with* me.
Even when I don't see him,
Even when I don't hear him,
Even when I don't feel him,
I know he is here.

Jesus is *for* me.
Helping me in my faith struggles—
Fluctuating emotions, pain, confusion, weakness,
and temptations;
He never condemns.

Jesus is *for* you.
I'm sharing my songs and verses—
My journey with Jesus in the valley of tears because
I want you to know the joy Jesus gives.

Blessed are those whose strength is in you,
    whose hearts are set on pilgrimage.

—Psalm 84:5 (NIV)

When they walk through the Valley of Weeping,
    it will become a place of refreshing springs.

—Psalm 84:6

THE VALLEY
OF TEARS

Darkness, confusion,
Fear, anxiety,
Loneliness,
Injury, pain, exhaustion,
Betrayal, injustice,
Sickness, loss,
Depression, despair,
Death—

She did not want to go there.
    Or remember.
How could it be "a place of refreshing"?
She did not believe it.

Gradually,
    as she learned to lean on Jesus,
This pilgrim discovered he was true.

And I am certain that God, who began the good work within you, will continue his work until it is finally finished on the day when Christ Jesus returns.

—Philippians 1:6

MY JOURNEY

I am traveling on a journey;
Wholeness is my goal.
Christ is my companion;
He cleansed and saved my soul.

Sometimes the road is rocky.
Sometimes the path is steep.
But Jesus' eye is on me;
He does not go to sleep.

And when I fall and stumble,
He redeems my mistake.
He never condemns me.
He never will forsake

His child, whom He has chosen,
His bride, whom He has called;
Someday I'll stand before Him,
Pure—without one fault!

We all have wandered away like sheep;
*   each of us has gone his own way.*
But the Lord has put on him the punishment
*   for all the evil we have done.*

—Isaiah 56:3 (NCV)

LOST AND BRUISED

I don't know what is wrong today,
Just where my heart has gone astray,
Just when and how I have wandered off,
But Lord, again, this lamb is lost.

I can feel the bramble stick,
And I don't know which path to pick
But most of all I hurt inside;
I so deeply miss my Guide.

Eating dust is terribly dry;
A drop of water, I can't buy.
Soon my strength and voice will end.
Please hear me Jesus, come again.

Come! In your mercy bind
Every bruise. Let me find
Within your arms sweet rest;
Teach me Jesus, what is best.

God saved you by his grace when you believed.
And you can't take credit for this; it is a gift from God.
Salvation is not a reward for the good things we have
done, so none of us can boast about it.

—Ephesians 2:8 - 9

Be energetic in your life of salvation, reverent and
sensitive before God. That energy is God's energy,
an energy deep within you, God himself willing and
working at what will give him the most pleasure.

—Philippians 2:12-13 (MSG)

CONFIDENCE

I haven't reached perfection yet.
There are many things still to correct,
But I can live contentedly
Because I know God speaks to me.

Perfection is His work, not mine.
I have His peace, the Spirit's sign,
And with this knowledge I can grow.
I need not fret and struggle so.

I'll walk with Him obediently,
Trust the Spirits' work in me,
Praise Him for His endless grace,
And someday see Him face to face.

Portraits

of

Grief

"Not so, my lord," Hannah replied, "I am a woman who is deeply troubled. I have not been drinking wine or beer; I was pouring out my soul to the Lord. Do not take your servant for a wicked woman; I have been praying here out of my great anguish and grief.

—1 Samuel 1:15-16 (NIV)

UNDIGNIFIED

Grief is not neat and orderly.
   I'd like her to be.
I want to assign her a time and a space.
She doesn't agree.

Paying no attention to the clock,
She interrupts me at unexpected times and in unexpected ways,
   Never saying, "Please!"

A demanding and impatient child,
She will not calm down until I give in to her.
Then, in just a few minutes,
She curls up and goes to sleep.

I return to neat and orderly.
It's not like it used to be.
For some reason, I have more peace.

Neat and orderly is still part of me,
But she's not so hard on me.

Having given up perfection,
She treats me with affection.

But when Peter saw the wind and the waves,
he became afraid and began to sink. He shouted,
"Lord, save me!"

Immediately Jesus reached out his hand and
caught Peter. Jesus said, "Your faith is small.
Why did you doubt?"

—Matthew 14:30-31 (NCV)

GRIEF IS LIKE WALKING ON A STORMY SEA

On some days I fear I will drown,
Yet I'm finding I have some control of it.

During an unpredictable tear-filled dip
I can cry, "Help!"
Reach out.

Grip the outstretched arm and firm hand of Jesus
Gradually, my anxiety decreases.

In moments when I'm feeling annoyed,
In the distance, I see a peak of joy.

I am not yet ready to go there,
Neither am I sinking.
Step-by-step, my faith is growing.

When you go through deep waters,
    I will be with you.
When you go through rivers of difficulty,
    you will not drown.
When you walk through the fire of oppression,
    you will not be burned up;
        the flames will not consume you.
For I am the Lord, your God,
    the Holy One of Israel, your Savior.

—Isaiah 43:2-3

GOD IS PRESENT

In the river of my mixed emotions, Jesus remains by my side.
With unchanging devotion, He
    Puts up with my anger,
    Accepts my tears,
    Allows me to doubt,
    Permits me to question.

In the river of my mixed emotions, Jesus remains by my side.
Never threatened by grief expressions, He
    Doesn't scold me
    Doesn't become anxious
    Doesn't say, "Now, hurry through it".

My grace is enough; it's all you need.

My strength comes into its own in your weakness.

—2 Corinthians 12:9 (MSG)

FOCUS

In the mixture of moments—
  Pain and pleasure,
Keep Christ as your focus.
  Keep him as your treasure.

He gives to his loved ones
  Grace in right measure;
Proportionately gives;
  He's a wise assessor.

When he is our focus;
  He is our treasure,
Joy becomes permanent.
  Pain's an erasure.

A friend loves you all the time,

and a brother helps in time of trouble.

—Proverbs 17:17 (NCV)

EMBRACE GRIEF

Do it gently. Do it kindly.
Do it wisely. Do it slowly.

When feeling sad, don't quickly flee,
Soothe yourself with a cup of tea.

If you don't face your painful memory,
If you force a smile of bravery,

It will show up later on.
You will have no happy song.

Allow yourself some time to cry.
Don't pretend it is fun to die.

When feeling happy, put on red.
Celebrate the joy you had.

Cling to memories that made you laugh.
Write a descriptive paragraph;

Share it with a compassionate friend
Who will hear and understand.

All this may take some time and work.
(Don't cover up what occurred)

Trust the friends you know can help you,
Ask them to join you in your venue—

Site of comfort, place of safety,
Take your time. Don't be hasty.

Admit to your pain or anger.
Let Jesus always be your anchor.

Safe

Stoop down and reach out to those who are oppressed.
Share their burdens, and so complete Christ's law.

—Galatians 6:2 (MSG)

HOW DO I KNOW WHEN I'VE GRIEVED ENOUGH?

People grieve loss differently.
Each of us proceeds in our own unique way.

Some of us seem to move very quickly.
We go from denial to acceptance
   Without skipping a beat;

Others of us appear to ignore grief stages.
   If it were less defined for us, we might grieve more easily.

I don't want another "recipe" or different directions.
I want a friend who will listen
   Without writing an assessment;

Someone who will turn off their timer and
   Not interrupt.
A friend whose prayer is not a prescription;

Someone who can stay, handle my silence, and
   Not be afraid of my anger and violence.

I want someone who refuses to give me
   Trite answers.
A friend who will not go to sleep while I'm talking,

I want someone who won't compare my experience with theirs—
Unless I invite them to share their story;

I want someone who listens with an ear turned to Jesus,
In their presence, I could sense His love and peace.

If I had a friend like the one I've described,
I think I'd know when I've grieved enough.

Resistance

All that I know now is partial and incomplete, but then I will know everything completely, just as God now knows me completely.

—1 Corinthians 13:12

WE PRETEND

We live in a time of incompleteness—
Every morning, death comes out to greet us.

We try to cover up her face.
Our pretense does not replace

The person missing at our table
We just spin another fable.

Yet we know, we all know,
Someday, we will be the missing one.

Because God's children are human beings—made of flesh and blood—the Son also became flesh and blood. For only as a human being could he die, and only by dying could he break the power of the devil, who had the power of death. Only in this way could he set free all who have lived their lives as slaves to the fear of dying.

—Hebrews 2:14-15

WE LIVE IN FEAR

What fearful people
You and I

Afraid of shadows
Afraid to die

Death is a shadow
Not something to fear

We close the door to life
Hide behind the shadow

But God finds us there
And gently leads us back to Light

He is Substance
Not shadow.

"I wish my suffering could be weighed

and my misery put on scales.

My sadness would be heavier than the sand of the seas.

No wonder my words seem careless

—Job 6:1-2 (NCV)

DISSONANCE

After the funeral people go home.
Does that mean their grieving is done?

For some it seems so. I don't hear them say
Anything more than "she went away"!

They talk of memories that brought them gladness.
What do they do with their sadness?

If they bury their anger and bottle their tears,
Does that mean those feelings disappear?

They go back to their jobs and act like it's over.
Don't lose their temper, have perfect composure.

Their friends tell them how well they are doing.
Is this really true? Who are they fooling?

Are they trying to be "holy"? Trying to look good?
Just acting in ways they were told they should?

Is this the way sorrow ceases?
Is this what it means to act like Jesus?

Will not the world think we are fake?
How will they know we feel their ache—

Loneliness, pain, grief, and despair--
When we smile and say, "I've not been there".

You make known to me the path of life;
you will fill me with joy in your presence,
with eternal pleasures at your right hand.

—Psalm 16:11 (NIV)

DISTRACTION

Sometimes this pathway of life is confusing.
Lord, help me pay attention,

Not come up with some new invention—
A substitute for your direction.

Even when the pathway is clear,
I stumble and veer from it,

Giving in to an impulse of the moment,
Or following a dysfunctional habit.

Jesus, I want to stay on it.
Become a person of integrity,

Someone you can trust.
I want the pleasure and joy you promise.

Keep me from collecting worthless coins,
From vendors who make deceitful promises;

Surrendering to them my money and time,
Having nothing left to offer you.

Keep placing the pathway in front of me.
Help me align my thoughts with your words

So that my feet follow through,
I accomplish the work you designed me to do.

There is a time for everything,
*   and everything on earth has its special season.*

There is a time to be born
*   and a time to die*

—Ecclesiastes 3:1-2 (NCV)

DENIAL

We do not know when death will come.
We do not choose that day.
Most of us just try to live our life
And put that thought away.

But when a neighbor or a friend
Is taken suddenly, by
   Fire,
    Flood,
  Or gun—

We wonder in our hearts
Why them?
Why them and
Why not me?

For I have traveled down that road.
I have slept at night
Unconscious of some danger;
Sometimes, I've lacked foresight.

What would I do if I could know
Death was close to me?
If I could know my time was short,
Would I live differently?

Where would I go? What would I do?
How would I spend my time?
What will I do about today?
That alone is mine.

I'm sure now I'll see God's goodness
    in the exuberant earth.
Stay with God!
    Take heart. Don't quit.
I'll say it again:
    Stay with God.

—Psalm 27:13 (MSG)

STRUGGLING TO ACCEPT IT

Last night, we got the phone call.
"She has cancer."
"It's not true!" I said.
And I kept on playing my board game.

On the way to bed, I heard the words, again.
"She has cancer."
"It's not true." I said.

In the morning, the words woke up.
"She has cancer."
"It's not true." I said.
I rolled over and covered my head.

The words were still there.
"She has cancer."
"This can't be true." I said.
"I am old. She is young. It isn't fair."

I got up and wrote the words out on paper.
"She has cancer."
Suddenly, the pen in my hand took off like a torpedo.
It covered those words with black circles of ink.
"It's not true," I said.

The tears in my eyes uncovered the lie I was telling myself.
My heart and my mind, at least in that moment, believed:

"She has cancer."

I understood—
My denial won't change it.
My anger won't heal her.

I prayed—
Jesus, show me what I can do
Help me still believe you are good.

Glimpses

of
Reality

*God formed Man out of dirt from the ground
and blew into his nostrils the breath of life.
The Man came alive—a living soul!*

—Genesis 2:7 (MSG)

*While we live in this body, we have burdens, and we
groan. We do not want to be naked, but we want to be
clothed with our heavenly home. Then this body that
dies will be fully covered with life.*

—2 Corinthians 5:4 (NCV)

FROM DUST TO LIFE

It's from dust that we arise
And to dust that we return

Is this all there is of us?
If it is, why make a fuss?

About positions and possessions
About performance and impressions

About the color of our skin
About the tribe that we are in

It's from dust that we arise
And to dust that we return

In between our birth and death
We each have a few short breaths

It might be eight; it might be eighty
Either way, we're not too weighty

It's from dust that we arise
It's from dust that we arise

It would be sad to think of this
If I believed that's all there is

Jesus tells me that there's more
He opened up heaven's door

Though from dust we arise
And to dust we return

It's not in dust that we remain
When Christ returns, we will gain

A body free from earthly chains
In which righteousness remains

When Christ returns we'll be free
Dust is not our identity

Freedom

Demas has deserted me because he loves the things of this life.

—2 Timothy 4:10

LIFE IS A SERIES OF GOOD-BYES

Some are easy.
Some are hard.

The easiest good-byes are the ones in which
I've made no commitment of time,
  money, energy or love.

The hardest good-byes are the ones in which
  no one cries and no one speaks.

I am left dangling
      by a half-cut thread
      to a relationship that's decayed.
But no one acknowledges it.

Sometimes I am called to say "goodbye"
  to the things and people I love the most,
in order to say "hello"
  to the God who loves me best.

When the people I love the most
  love me enough to talk to me about that goodbye,
I feel comforted, and they do too.

When they turn their back and walk away
  It's so much harder.

Our lifetime is seventy years
  or, if we are strong, eighty years.
But the years are full of hard work and pain.
  They pass quickly, and then we are gone. Teach us
how short our lives really are
  so that we may be wise.

—Psalm 90:10, 12 (NCV)

NO TIME TO WASTE

"Good-bye" to the womb.
"Hello" to the grave.

The space in-between is a few short breaths.
We tell ourselves time is endless.

Fritter away our days and hours
As if our breath will never cease.

Even in our senior years,
We delude ourselves, believe we'll have

Another decade; when that ends
We add another one onto it.

Time speeds up as the years go by;
We still don't comprehend it will end—

"Maybe for others," I said. "Not for me."
Then *one day*, I believed what I'd heard—

My time on this earth truly is limited.
I stopped frittering away my hours and days.

When my turn comes to go to the grave,
I want to have finished the work I've been given.

When it's my time to rise from the grave,
I want to hear Jesus' words, "Well done."

Even youths get tired and weary;
even strong young men clumsily stumble
But those who wait for the Lord's help find renewed
strength;
they rise up as if they had eagles' wings,
they walk without getting tired.

—Isaiah 40:30-31 (NET)

JESUS STRENGTHEN ME

Jesus,
Strengthen me when I feel
Weak and I no more desire
To love my neighbor as myself;
Jesus, hold me tighter.

Wrap me in your arms of love
And fill my soul with laughter;
When my heart dwells in that place
The storms outside don't matter.

I'm not troubled or disturbed
By words of opposition;
I respond with gentle strength
'Cause you are my protection.

Jesus,
Strengthen me when I am
Old and I feel too tired
To love my neighbor as myself;
I know it's still required.

Wrap me in your arms of love
And fill my soul with laughter;
For when my heart dwells in that place
The storms outside don't matter.

I'm not worried or disturbed
By a loss of memory;
I have confidence and joy
'Cause your Spirit still is in me.

Jesus,
Strengthen me when I feel
Sad and I can't stop weeping
About the destruction of the virus,
As through the world it's sweeping.

Show me, Lord, what you are doing.
Teach me how to intercede.
Give me confidence you answer prayer
As with your Spirit, I plead.

Open my eyes and let me see
What this war looks like to you;
Give me knowledge, insight, wisdom
That I may share in what you do.

Slashes

of

Pain

Nothing in all creation is hidden from God's sight.

—Hebrews 4:13 (NIV)

GOD KNOWS

Lord, what is this pain so deep within
That brings me to your throne again?
I know I've felt your power to heal
There's still a hurt I can't conceal.

You know me well, and right will do,
Again I yield my heart to you.
I'm crying but there's no despair
I feel your arms, I know your care.

And in your time you'll show me why
It is enough, I need not try
To make excuse or tell a lie,
Lord, you know what is awry.

Your human heart with God combined
Knows every naked thought of mine,
And in your presence I can stand.
You intercede with pierced hand.

Exhausted by my tears I feel,
Still your comfort is so real.
Oh perfect surgeon, mend my heart
Make me true in every part.

I will be happy and rejoice in your faithfulness,
because you notice my pain
and you are aware of how distressed I am.

—Psalm 31:7 (NET)

JESUS IS HERE

When pain is crushing, my heart is breaking,
My faithful Savior does not forsake me.
Alone in stillness, I hear him calling
His steadfast mercy keeps me from falling.

I praise my Savior. His grace sustains me.
I praise my Father. His love upholds me.
I praise the Spirit. His peace surrounds me.
My God is faithful. He does not leave me.

When in the battle, my strength is fleeting,
And in the conflict, I'm meeting failure,
I bring to Jesus my fear and sorrow;
He gives me songs of joy and courage.

I praise my Savior. His grace sustains me.
I praise my Father. His love upholds me.
I praise the Spirit. He surrounds me.
My God is faithful. He does not leave me.

You have turned my mourning into joyful dancing.
You have taken away my clothes of mourning and clothed me with joy

—Psalm 30:11

CHRONIC PAIN

It's with me forever.
Medications don't work.
What my doctors suggest
Often makes things worse.

It's a constant reminder
I'm a flesh and blood person
Dependent on others—
Not the ruler of heaven.

I can choose to resent it.
And die in stagnation;
Or I can accept it
And make adaptations.

I can gripe and complain,
Focus on my misery,
Or give it to Jesus;
He always is with me.

He takes what seems useless,
My weakness and my pain,
And converts it to song;
I live in joy, not shame.

He will wipe away every tear from their eyes, and death will not exist any more—or mourning, or crying, or pain, for the former things have ceased to exist.

—Revelation 21:4 (NET)

SHORT-TERM

Pain is but a temporary thing.
Though, for me, it feels permanent,
Its time is limited.
Its end is certain.

Though, I tremble beneath its grip,
I do not succumb to its intimidation.
I do not surrender to fear.
I do not give in to guilt.

Pain is a temporary thing.
Though, for me, it feels permanent,
Its time is limited.
Its end is certain.

Though I am not yet healed,
I am confident I will be.
Jesus declared it.
He's preparing me to receive it.

Pain is a temporary thing.
Though, for me, it feels permanent,
Its time is limited.
Its end is certain.

Don't panic. I'm with you.

There's no need to fear for I'm your God.

I'll give you strength. I'll help you.

I'll hold you steady, keep a firm grip on you.

—Isaiah 41:10 (MSG)

RED LIGHT

Pain is simply a red light.
I don't have to get uptight,

Just slow down and figure out
What that signal's all about.

Is it some imagined fear?
Or is it danger lurking near?

If to Jesus I stay close,
He will deliver me from both.

Fear makes pain feel much worse.
So does every grudge I nurse.

Pain's a red light sent from God
To tell me it is wise to stop.

It's wise to stop, not block that sound.
I may need to turn around,

Confess some attitude as sin,
Stop a project or begin,

Rest my body and my soul.
In God's time, I will be whole.

If I listen and obey,
I will feel great joy someday.

Meanwhile, I will not despair.
Jesus truly, truly cares.

He's my Shepherd and my Guide.
In his Grace I will abide.

Grace

Now that we know what we have—Jesus, this great High Priest with ready access to God—let's not let it slip through our fingers. We don't have a priest who is out of touch with our reality. He's been through weakness and testing, experienced it all—all but the sin. So let's walk right up to him and get what he is so ready to give. Take the mercy, accept the help.

—Hebrews 4:14-16 (MSG)

UNENDING EMPATHY

When pain would take my breath away;
It persists night and day.
I will not increase my agony
By listening to anxiety.

Too often, I've made that choice,
Blocking out the Spirit's voice; he reminds me
I'm held in the arms of love.
All is well.

My Shepherd is not unaware of my pain.
He walks with me as I go through it—
Understanding,
Weeping,
Interceding.

Loneliness

Jonathan became one in spirit with David, and he loved him as himself.

—1 Samuel:18:1 (NIV)

I MISS YOU SO MUCH

My sister, my twin, my friend,
I miss you so much!

You intuitively knew my thoughts—
    needed few words to understand my heart
We laughed, cried, crawled, walked, talked, jumped, ran, hid,
baked, cooked, cleaned,
    prayed, and sang together.

Always, we sang.
Always, we were together.

Today, I'm remembering the song we sang
    when we were eight, and
    when we were eighteen—
Before we graduated and went to different colleges.

Always, we sang.
Always, we were together.

We sang the same song
    when we were together
In separate places—
Your body was slowly dying

Always, we sang.
Always, we are together.
After the phone call, I cried.

My sister, my twin, my friend,
  I missed you so much.

You intuitively knew my thoughts—
    needed few words to understand my heart
We laughed, cried, crawled, walked, talked,
jumped, ran, hid, baked, cooked, cleaned,
    prayed, and sang together.

Always, we sang.
Always, we were together.

Today, I'm crying, again.
My sister, my twin, my friend,
    I miss you so much!

A NURSERY RHYME MEMORY

You've been gone three months, Mother.
Three months, today.
The child inside of me is still crying,
"Come back, Mama, come back!"

This morning as I walked the
Uphill side of the block, I looked
Up from the pavement and saw the moon above the trees.
Suddenly I heard your voice . . .

"Hey diddle, diddle, the cat and the fiddle,
The cow jumped over the moon,
The little dog laughed to see such a sport
And the dish ran away with the spoon."

It was as if you were walking beside me,
Reciting that nursery rhyme
The memory of your happy laughing voice
Was so strong I felt I could have touched you.

It's hard to think of you as not here.
Maybe you are on vacation and you will
Come back. No, you've gone away.
You're far away, far over the moon.

The room was filled with widows who were weeping and showing him the coats and other clothes Dorcas had made for them.

—Acts 9:39

MISSING NANA

There is no snow this winter,
No soft wavy drifts crowning the receding brow
    gone from my sight.

No snatches of blue sky wedded with sunshine,
    peeking through fogged windows
to welcome me home.

No aged canary, sweetly whistling a Mozart tune,
    waiting with open wings
to gather me under her breast.

The brown leather rocker,
    once warmed by a portly lap and freckled with
gingersnap crumbs,
greets me with silence.

The face of the mantle clock,
    once lovingly smudged by chubby fingers dipped
in strawberry jam,
No longer chimes for three o'clock tea.

There is no snow this winter,
    just memories of drifts and mounds of photographs
I can't shovel through

If your gift is to encourage others, be encouraging.

—Romans 12:8

IRONY

Lonely is a feeling I don't like to have;
For that feeling, I've found no nippy salve.

I tried chocolate. It didn't work.
I tried avoidance. That made it worse.

Lonely is a feeling that's hard to share,
Because when I'm lonely, no one's there.

Even though people may be around,
The problem's there. This I've found—

It's hard to speak "lonely" out loud,
'Cause it was a feeling called "not allowed.

Even if my father and mother abandon me,
the Lord will hold me close.

—Psalm 27:10 (NLT)

A FATHER CAN'T DIE

Writing a letter is just not the same.
On the envelope is only one name.

Mr. and Mrs., it always has been,
Now it's just Mrs.

No, it can't be.
A father can't die

A dream—
Maybe it was a dream,
A wax figure dressed in his clothes;
It looked nothing like him.

No, it can't be
A father can't die.

Mr., come back!
Come back to Mrs.
Come back to me.
You left without saying goodbye.

Writing a letter is just not the same.
On the envelope is only one name.

He will wipe away every tear from their eyes, and death will not exist anymore—or mourning, or crying, or pain, for the former things have ceased to exist.

—Revelation 21:4 (NET)

Look, a time is coming—and has come—when you will be scattered, each one to his own home, and I will be left alone. Yet I am not alone, because my Father is with me.

—John 16:32 (NET)

LONELINESS IS

My companion,
Who, in silence, walks with me;
It's a sad, familiar feeling,
Often felt when friends I see.

Arms around me help to comfort;
For a moment, I'm set free,
That painful longing leaves.
I feel love's mystery.

A listening heart, words of wisdom,
Laughter soon replaces tears,
My spirit feels united.

Loneliness, I cease to fear.
Quickly, though, that moment passes,
Lonesomeness envelops me.
Then, I pause and remember
One who died upon a tree—

My loneliness cannot compare
With the cup that Jesus bore,
Rejected, deserted, abandoned by all,
My sadness cannot compare!

In all of my loneliness, he's been present,
Whether I've seen him or not;
He will faithfully remain 'til sorrow is absent,
Whether I feel him or not!

In his presence, one day, there will be
No more shadows that sever.
Then, I will know as I'm fully known.
Separation will be banished forever!

No shadows

The Spirit and the bride say, "Come." Let anyone who hears this say, "Come." Let anyone who is thirsty come. Let anyone who desires drink freely from the water of life.

—Revelation 22:17

HOMECOMING

When we come to death's dark valley
We need not walk alone.
God, himself, will walk beside us.
He came down from heaven's throne,

Lived a perfect life among us,
Then died for what we'd done—
For our omissions and imperfections;
By this, his love was shown.

Yes, he died but he has risen
And now prepares for us a home,
Where all pain and tears will vanish,
Death will never come.

Today, he gives the invitation—
"Let all the thirsty come.
With my righteousness I'll clothe you;
I bought you for my own."

Jesus calls you, for he loves you;
You need never walk alone.
He will be your light in each dark valley;
Then, will lead you home.

Friends
Who
Comfort

As the mountains surround Jerusalem,

the Lord surrounds his people

now and forever.

—Psalm 125:2 (NCV)

ASSURANCE

When clouds cover the mountains,
Do you doubt they are there?

When you cannot feel my presence,
Do you doubt my care?

Though the mountains be removed
And cast into the sea,

I have promised I will never
Depart from thee.

Why, my soul, are you downcast?

Why so disturbed within me?

Put your hope in God,

for I will yet praise him,

my Savior and my God

—Psalm 42:5 (NIV)

A PSALM

Depression
   Like waves of a swirling tide
Threatens to engulf
   My soul

For awhile, I fight
   Against the current
My endurance is limited, my
   Struggling ends.

"Rescue me, God! I pray.
   He does not. I
Sink into the darkness.

He does not allow me to remain there, forever.
Light surrounds me.

By faith
   I cling to his promises
He shows me treasures in the sea—
   Unexpected JOY

God blesses those who mourn for they shall be comforted.

—Matthew 5:4

CAN WE CRY OPENLY?

These were the instructions Daddy gave—
Show no sadness at my grave,

Those who weep show unbelief.
I request a quiet grief.

Honor me and bring no tears.
Do not shame me by your fears.

How could I who've wept through life
Not feel sorrow at this knife?

Should missing him not bring me pain?
I held back my tears, did not complain;

Then, alone, after the funeral,
Released those tears in a foam pillow—

That pillow gave me no smile or hug.
I felt alone. It wasn't enough.

Why can't we weep openly?
Must we hide our pain and flee?

Is this truly the Christian way?
I wonder what our founder would say?

Jesus wept.

—John 11:35

He showed them his hands and feet. And how wonderful was their joy as they saw their Lord!

—John 20:20 (TLB)

JESUS WEPT

Jesus wept
When he saw death
Openly
Not with shame

Jesus wept
When he saw death
His heart was sensitive
He loved his friend

Jesus wept
When he saw death
He still does
When he sees us

He feels our pain
Is not ashamed
To take our hand
Walk there again

He stays right here
On the path of grief
And wipes our tears
When we cry

Jesus wept
When he saw death
But not for long
He conquered it

Rose from the grave
Returned to joy
And we will too
If we look into his eyes.

JOY,
Not death
Will be the end
When we ascend!

A friend loves at all times,

and a brother is born for a time of adversity.

—Proverbs 17:17 (NIV)

NOT ALONE

In my dark, troubled, season of grief,
You are a friend to me.

You notice I'm alone,
Extend your arm and
Place your hand close to mine,

Offering, not demanding, I touch it.
After a while, I do. We connect.
Tears form in my eyes,
And in yours

In my dark, troubled, season of grief,
You are a friend to me.

You notice I'm alone,
Look into my eyes and
Without words speak to me,

Offering, not demanding, I talk.
After a while, I do. We connect
A tiny smile forms on my face,
And on yours

In my dark, troubled, season of grief,
You are a friend to me.
I am not alone.

Rejoice with those who rejoice, weep with those who weep.

—Romans 15:12 (NET)

PERMISSION

"I read your poem.
    It brought tears to my eyes."

Tears to her eyes?
    (That's what she said.)

But
Crying is not something she does,
    (in the open).

Although, once or twice
    through sideways glance,
I've seen her wipe her nose and
    brush a tear from her eye.

But
Crying is not something she does.
    (in the open).

It's my job to protect her from it,
    (make her happy)

Crying is something I do
But,
    (not in the open).

"It's all right, Mother.
You can cry as much as you want to.
I cry, sometimes, too."

And there are different ways that God works through people but the same God. God works in all of us in everything we do. Something from the Spirit can be seen in each person, for the common good.

—1 Corinthians 12: 6-7 (NCV)

RECEIVE
COMMUNITY GRACE

What would wipe away my gloom?
I could make up a happy tune,

Write another rhyming verse,
Or organize my flowered purse.

It was my daughter's gift to me—
Special, she will always be!

I could design a photo card;
It would not be very hard.

Have my neighbor cut my bangs
So in my eyes they would not hang.

Invite her to have tea with me;
Find out on what we can agree.

Take myself on a very long walk;
Listen closely to my "self-talk".

Evaluate the truthfulness
Of my inner messages.

If I have blown my diet
It's best not to deny it;

Confess failure without shame
And better understand my game;

Come out from my hiding place;
Receive God's embrace of grace.

Barriers

Be careful of false prophets. They come to you looking gentle like sheep, but they are really dangerous like wolves.

—Matthew 7:15 (NCV)

CURIOSITY DEVOID
OF COMPASSION

Like a ruthless dentist who performs
A root canal without anesthetic
Is the therapist who uses technique
Apart from a caring relationship.

Only the person acquainted with sorrow
Can safely handle the laser of truth,
Targeting decay in the core of my being
Without slashing my wounded heart.

If the grief I'm experiencing is necessary
To keep me from becoming insensitive,
Then, my Father, I accept it with joy—
Knowing your Grace will sustain me;

But if it is an instrument sent to destroy
Me, I will vehemently refuse it. I want
Never to grow callous and indifferent
To the pain of those you call me to love.

He went to the Pharisee's house and sat down at the dinner table. Just then a woman of the village, the town harlot, having learned that Jesus was a guest in the home of the Pharisee, came with a bottle of very expensive perfume and stood at his feet, weeping, raining tears on his feet. Letting down her hair, she dried his feet, kissed them, and anointed them with the perfume. When the Pharisee who had invited him saw this, he said to himself, "If this man was the prophet I thought he was, he would have known what kind of woman this is who is falling all over him."

—Luke 7:36-39 (MSG)

SHE OPENED HER HEART TO A PHARISEE

He looked at his watch, cleared his throat, and
Said to her—

"I think that poem is nice,
 Now, where was I?
 Oh! It's getting late.

I have another appointment to keep.
Maybe you could come back next week."

It was an inconvenient time for this woman to weep.
She went home and put her poem on a back shelf.

Do you think your words are convincing

—Job 6:26

AM I INVISIBLE?

Is there anyone who will hear my cry?
Is there anyone who will understand my pain?
Is there anyone who will weep with me?

For a moment,
You stand and look.
You say nothing.
Your eyes don't blink.
Your feet don't move.

Then, you hand me a "Gospel tract."
Wish me a "good day."
Turn and walk away.

How can I believe you care about me?

My days are over.
  My hopes have disappeared.
  My heart's desires are broken.

—Job 17:11

UNHEARD

In this world where pain is real
Sometimes, we hurt too much to feel;

So we conceal our brokenness
Behind a mask of happiness—

The smile and laughter that we bring
Is our response to everything!

When someone senses dissonance,
We firmly claim our innocence

And quickly move to safer ground—
Where tears and frowns are never found.

All these people are known for their faith, but none of them received what God had promised.

—Hebrews 11:39

QUESTIONS

My sister is gradually dying
Not in minutes or days but years
I fear if I visit her I will find another
Part of her has disappeared

I don't want to believe it
I don't want to see it.
It seems so unfair
It seems so unjust.

There's nothing I can do to stop it
I wish I could forget about it
I'm not ready to go there, today
Wait! She's my sister. I can't stay away

I don't want to believe it
I don't want to see it.
It seems so unfair
It seems so unjust.

I don't have the faith to pray
That this disease will go away
I wish I did but I confess
It's not the miracle I can embrace

I don't want to believe it
I don't want to see it.
It seems so unfair
It seems so unjust.

If I put this struggle into words
Perhaps I'll gain some clarity
About what faith really means
When I can see no miracle

I read it years ago in the King James
Faith is the evidence of things not seen—
Faith is the evidence that's *not* evident
Is that what this means for me?

Faith

"You were like a woman whose husband left her,
*   and you were very sad.*
You were like a wife who married young
*   and then her husband left her.*
But the Lord called you to be his,"
*   says your God.*

—Isaiah 54:6 (NCV)

UNBELIEF

I was worn out with fear and doubt;
Yet, I could not figure out
How to escape the thing in me
That kept my mind in slavery.

It was not a chain put on
Me by someone else, just my song—
It was my own song of unbelief
That kept me in a state of grief.

Then one day, Jesus came!
He set me free, broke my chain!
This was the truth he spoke to me:
"I've loved you from eternity."

Now at last I understand
I was wanted. I was planned.
Jesus healed me, made me whole.
I have a purpose and a goal.

Free from fear, guilt, and shame
I serve my Lord and for him, claim
Through prayer, the things he speaks to me,
Things, which only faith can see;

Not toys of silver or of gold,
Which tarnish and collect green mold—
But gifts incorruptible,
Rewards indestructible.

I was worn out with fear and doubt.
Jesus knew what it was about
This was the truth he spoke to me:
"I've loved you from eternity."

Loved

"When we were unable to help ourselves, at the right time, Christ died for us, although we were living against God. Very few people will die to save the life of someone else. Although perhaps for a good person someone might possibly die. But God shows his great love for us in this way: Christ died for us while we were still sinners.

—Romans 5:6-8 (NCV)

INTROSPECTION

Just as I am
I come to you, Lord.
I don't understand the confusion within.
(Why I am guilty, how I have sinned.)

Search my heart.
Not in a condemning, introspective manner,
    As I would do;
Instead,
With the sweetness of grace.

I've taken too many painful
Trips into the past,
Discovering only despair;

Correct my distorted vision.
Cut my attachment to falsehood.
Bond my soul with truth.

Anger

A gentle answer will calm a person's anger, but an unkind answer will cause more anger.

—Proverbs 15:1 (NCV)

A TANKER FULL OF ANGER

I'm a tanker full of anger.
Don't get in front of me.
My throttle's fully open;
If I were you, I'd flee.

I'm a tanker full of anger,
Roaring down life's highway;
My brakes are not working.
I think you better pray.

I'm a tanker full of anger.
It's a very heavy load.
If I don't dump some of it,
I'm afraid I'll explode.

I'm a tanker full of anger.
Unlit dynamite,
I was created over time
By things that were not right:

Prejudice and pain,
Injustice and neglect,
Losses that I suffered,
Failures to protect,

Beliefs and attitudes
That pushed me away,
I'm a tanker full of anger.
I wish that you would stay—

I wish you would help me
Unload successfully,
Not injure self or others,
Handle grief effectively.

*Better to be slow to anger than to be a mighty warrior,
and one who controls his temper is better than one who
captures a city.*

—Proverbs 16:32 (NET)

*The Spirit produces the fruit of love, [and] . . . self-
control.*

—Galatians 5:22-23 (NCV)

FURY

Like a stallion untamed that will not relent,
I'm destroying myself with anger unspent.

Bound for so long, I'm afraid to run free—
Afraid my rage will be stronger than me.

I want someone who will listen attentively.
I've conditioned myself to no longer see

The wide open door, a safe place to move out;
My heart still contains suspicion and doubt.

Those I could trust have all moved away.
I wanted to go but here I must stay.

Some I have sent, pretending of course
That I did not care; I'm filled with remorse.

Where can I turn to find help and hope?
I feel that I've reached the end of my rope.

Can anyone leash this fury within?
Teach me to walk in wholeness, not sin?

I want to grow up! I want to mature!
I will not go back! I cannot endure

Relationships where I feel like a worm,
I put myself down, with embarrassment squirm.

I want to be tamed, not in fear still run wild,
More deeply relate, not hide like a child.

I am tired and worn, and I do not know why,
But I want to be tamed before I must die.

Untamed

Jesus was sleeping at the back of the boat with his head on a cushion. The disciples woke him up, shouting, "Teacher, don't you care that we're going to drown?"

When Jesus woke up, he rebuked the wind and said to the waves, "Silence! Be still!" Suddenly the wind stopped, and there was a great calm. Then he asked them, "Why are you afraid? Do you still have no faith?"

The disciples were absolutely terrified. "Who is this man?" they asked each other. "Even the wind and waves obey him!"

—Matthew 14:38-41

EPILOGUE

Just like the fuming stallion, like the raging sea,
Anger rose like billows deep inside of me.

Despite all my knowledge, I could gain control.
I did not trust in others. I would not be consoled.

Then I remembered Jesus, who created me.
I listened to his voice; so gentle was he

My fear dissipated, My defense I let down.
I bowed my knees to his authority and crown.

Yes, Jesus has conquered the sea and also me.
Lord Jesus, calm each storm by your authority.

Then I will find rest! Then, I will be free!
By these I am tamed—your words of love to me.

Who may worship in your sanctuary, Lord?
  Who may enter your presence on your holy hill?
  Those who lead blameless lives and do what is right,
  speaking the truth from sincere hearts.

—Psalm 15: 1-2

DESIRING INTEGRITY

My anger is tied in with pride
So its expression I must hide.

For those who now admire me
Might change their minds

If they could see the thoughts I have,
How *mad* I feel.

But how I wish that I could deal
More openly with all my fears;

I'm not as nice as I might seem
I'm not as strong as I appear,

I'm not as confident as I might look.
(Although I've memorized God's book).

And in the night I often dream
Of being free—
Just being me;

I want to have integrity.
I want to grow in servanthood.
I want to *be,* not just look good.

When you are angry, do not sin, and be sure to stop being angry before the end of the day.

—Ephesians 4:26 (NCV)

ANGER IS A SIGNAL

How much easier it is, when during my day,
I pay attention to messages of anger.

When I disregard her, she silently
Sneaks into bed with me.

After a few hours, she interrupts my sleep,
Reminding me of someone I refused to forgive.

Anger, like pain, is not a solution.
It's a red signal light.

If I run too many red lights, sooner or later,
I'll collide with someone—

Someone a lot bigger
and a lot stronger than me!

The Lord is compassionate and merciful,
*   slow to get angry and filled with unfailing love.*

—Psalm 103:8

Don't copy the behavior and customs of this world, but
let God transform you into a new person by changing
the way you think. Then you will learn to know God's
will for you, which is good and pleasing and perfect.

—Romans 12:2

TRANSFORM ME

Spirit, make me slow to anger
Kind and patient, quicker thankful
More like Christ, my Lord and Savior
As for his purposes, I labor.

Spirit, make me slow to anger
I admit, it's not my nature
Since a child, I've been short-tempered
Gained attention in that way

Spirit, make me slow to anger
When I'm hurt, I yearn for vengeance
Never has it brought me closure
I feel worse when it is over

Spirit, make me slow to anger
Before reacting, help me listen
Hear your viewpoint and accept it
Always, you speak accurately

Spirit, make me slow to anger
Show me lies I love and clutch
I long for peace and unity
Bring order to my muddled mind

Spirit, make me slow to anger
Kind and patient, quicker thankful
More like Christ, my Lord and Savior
As for his purposes, I labor.

Turn
Around

If we love our brothers and sisters who are believers, it proves that we have passed from death to life. But a person who has no love is still dead.

—1 John 3:14

IT'S NOT JUST ABOUT ME

Yes, Jesus, I'm beginning to see
Life is not just about me
My feelings, my pain,
My sensitivity

Life and *Faith* are not just about me
It includes others.
Others hurt. Not just me.
Others have brothers and sisters

Parents die and children cry
Viruses invade the earth
Cruelty and evil reigns
Floods and fires sweep the globe

Yet what is dying on this earth
Will someday rise up from the grave
Jesus will raise us as he said,
There will be no sickness and no death

That's something that I *do* believe
That something, too, takes some faith
And when I think about that fact
With faith, I love. With faith, I act.

Faith is the evidence of things not seen
It's for the present in-between
When some are healed and some must wait
The book of Hebrews tells us about

The men and women who by faith
Were made strong in weakness
Were stoned and sawn in two
Were afflicted and mistreated

And these were commended for faith.
Sometimes, we also have to wait
Let's not give up; let's not retreat
Let's join our hands and sing.

Unity

*There is a path before each person that seems right,
    but it ends in death.*

—Proverbs 14:12

LOVING CONFRONTATION

I felt proud and happy
Until I looked in the mirror;
Truth was too painful
I didn't want to go there.

I continued my journey, ignoring sad Truth,
Pursuing pleasure, entertainment and mirth;
The image I saw did not go away;
God in his *Love* caused it to stay—

Happiness felt empty.
I couldn't sleep. I couldn't eat.
Success felt like loss
I admitted defeat,

I went back to the mirror,
Looked, again, at Truth,
Said, "I'll accept it.
"It might have some worth."

The image I saw suddenly changed
Ugliness left. Beauty arrived
I'm so thankful *Love* took time to
Convince me of *Truth* I'd declined.

"Anyone who listens to my teaching and follows it is wise, like a person who builds a house on solid rock. Though the rain comes in torrents and the floodwaters rise and the winds beat against that house, it won't collapse because it is built on bedrock. 26 But anyone who hears my teaching and doesn't obey it is foolish, like a person who builds a house on sand. When the rains and floods come and the winds beat against that house, it will collapse with a mighty crash."

—Matthew 7:24-27

SHAKE-UP

Yesterday, I saw Jesus.
His eyes looked straight through me.

I felt incredible pain.
Then, indescribable joy!

He completely demolished my house on the sand.
And severed my bond with a lie!

"Brothers and sisters, if someone is caught in a sin, you who live by the Spirit should restore that person gently. But watch yourselves, or you also may be tempted. Carry each other's burdens, and in this way you will fulfill the law of Christ."

—Galatians 6:1-3 (NIV)

BATTLE FOR INTEGRITY

When what we *do* receives a smile,
And who we *are* is overlooked,
We learn quite early how to play
The game that's called "Looking Good."

'Cause in this world, where gods of
Beauty, strength, and money reign,
Judgments fall on those who fail;
How could we say, "That's my fault"?

"This load is heavy. I need help!"
"I don't know how. I was afraid."
"I feel ashamed. I told a lie!"
Honesty would break the rules.

In "Looking Good" appearance counts;
We hide our flaws, our guilt, and shame.
And oft' design two separate lives—
One up front and one inside:

One at school and one at home
One at church and one at work
One with family, one with friends
One on Facebook, one offline.
 If too long we play this game,
We lose touch of who we are;
We lose sight of all our goals;
A deep sadness fills our souls.

"Looking Good" is hard to do;
What is *true* keeps leaking through.
"Looking Good" adds to shame;
"Looking Good" makes us blame;

In our mask, a crack appears;
We injure those that we hold dear.
Just like Clinton, Cruz, and Trump,
Under pressure, we erupt.

Then, with another choice, we're blessed:
Admit to our inward mess,
Or go right back and play the game.
Changing is *so* hard to do.

Unless we have a loving friend,
Who'll gently guide us, take our hand,
Who'll help us climb, but not control,
Who'll let us move at our own pace,

Who'll not reject us when we fall,
Yet will, with grace, our blunder's call,
And summon us to wisely choose
Internal goodness, not applause.

Unless we have a friend like this,
We may not leave our painful game.
It's just too hard; our path's ingrained.
We'll likely choose to stay the same.

How profound that God knows this!
How amazing that he choose
To come to earth and demonstrate
What it means to not pretend.

For Jesus, "Good" was not a game;
It was his true and shameless name.
He was himself and nothing more—
Nothing more and nothing less.

He had no guilt to cover up
He was the same, inside and out.
Never once did he bow down
To gods who called him to conform.

When we connect our hearts with his,
We find the strength to end our game.
And gradually he will impart
True goodness to our yielded hearts.

"O Lord, you have examined my heart
and know everything about me.
You know when I sit down or stand up.
You know my thoughts even when I'm far away."

—Psalm 139:1-2

SLOW ME DOWN

So swept away in business am I
I don't know what my inner thoughts are

How can I be so close to me
And not detect
Impurity—
Fear and pride that hide inside?

Holy Spirit, shine your Light on my heart
Show me what is garbage;
Help me throw it out with boldness and joy!

Show me what is worthy of keeping,
Gold you have placed there.
Refine it and show me who I can share it with

The father instantly cried out, "I do believe, but help me overcome my unbelief!"

—Mark 9:24

EVIDENCE ACCEPTED

Repentance moves us past survival
Into the joy of true revival,

In which God's Spirit comes with power;
The sick are healed and demons cower.

Every faithless heart and troubled mind
Comprehend, at last, that God is kind.

They believe God's words are plausible
And embrace what looks impossible

Forgiveness

And forgive us our debts,

as we also have forgiven our debtors.

—Matthew 6:12 (NIV)

STRUGGLING
TO FORGIVE

I can feel it in my stomach
I can feel it in my jaws
I can feel it in my backbone
And I think I have just cause

For the anger that consumes me
For the hatred I possess
But I am tortured by its presence
My soul can find no rest.

My soul is being devoured
I live in constant pain
I pray to God in heaven
But I cannot break the chain.

I must somehow choose forgiveness
I must somehow turn around
I must somehow stop reacting
But the way I have not found.

Can you understand my struggle?
Can you understand my grief?
Will you listen to my story?
Will you pray for my release?

But you desire honesty from the womb,
*   teaching me wisdom even there.*

—Psalm 51: 6

RESTORATION

Take some time for deep reflection.
Combined with journaling and prayer,
It will change your deep unconscious—
Restore love and order there.

Untie knots of resentment. They
Grip your lungs and steal your air,
Causing panic and exhaustion;
Your brain's designed for love not fear.

Renounce the vow that keeps you bound—
The oath you made to get revenge;
Gain freedom from the pain that grips
Your jaw and sets your teeth on edge.

Choose forgiveness. Ask for mercy.
Don't let anger become a wedge,
Separating you from others;
Make compassion your daily pledge.

Bless the people who have hurt you;
Include yourself if this you know—
Your self-talk is a poisonous brew.
It's time to end that toxic flow.

Take some time for deep reflection.
Combined with journaling and prayer,
It will change your deep unconscious—
Restore love and order there.

If we say we have no sin, we are fooling ourselves, and the truth is not in us. But if we confess our sins, he will forgive our sins, because we can trust God to do what is right. He will cleanse us from all the wrongs we have done. If we say we have not sinned, we make God a liar, and we do not accept God's teaching.

—1 John 1:8-10 (NCV)

SWAMP OF
UNFORGIVENESS

Grief always means the failure of
Someone, sometime, somewhere;

Often that someone is me.
That's not where I want the failure to be.

I prefer to think more about failures of others
(My father, mother, sisters, brothers,

Friends, neighbors, government, teachers)
Than I do about my own failures.

That makes me slow to forgive
And in misery, I live.

Stuck in memories of failures and injury,
My mind can't focus on tasks of the day.

Unforgiveness blocks the path to success.
It's a tangled web, a terrible mess.

God, I need help to sort all this out.
I want to take another route.

I'm tired of life in the swamp of unforgiveness,
It's too painful, too distressing, too exhausting,

Pull me out! Set me free!
God of grace, forgive me.

So just as sin ruled over all people and brought them to death, now God's wonderful grace rules instead, giving us right standing with God and resulting in eternal life through Jesus Christ our Lord.

—Romans 5:21

RECEIVING GRACE

I refused to receive the grace of forgiveness.
I could not forget my failures to
   love God, self, and others.

This practice blinded me.
It caused me to see
   my sins magnified in other faces.

The Spirit showed me this truth.
I confessed my arrogance,
   received grace, and was set free.

Love does not count up wrongs that have been done.

—1 Corinthians 13:5 (NCV)

So I say, let the Holy Spirit guide your lives. Then you won't be doing what your sinful nature craves.

—Galatians 5:16

BREAKTHROUGH

If your love's decreasing—
You are *not* greeting
Your brother and your sister with a smile—

Go back to Jesus.
Ask him the reason
You refuse to go the second mile

If your body is weary
And you feel teary,
You may find tempted to revile.

You can release resentment;
You can find contentment,
If you hang out with the Spirit for awhile

Compassion

He comforts us in all our troubles so that we can comfort others. When they are troubled, we will be able to give them the same comfort God has given us.

—2 Corinthians 1:4

BECOMING A COMFORTER

I look all around me
There's pain everywhere
My friends are all hurting
It's so hard to bear

How can I show them
That I really care?
When my heart is so heavy
I feel such despair

"Don't look at their wounds
Just look at my face
I've promised to heal them
Just trust in my grace

My child, come closer
Come closer to me
My comfort I'll give you
Then comfort you'll be"

Timothy, our brother, works with us for God and helps us tell people the Good News about Christ. We sent him to strengthen and encourage you in your faith.

—1 Thessalonians 3:2 (NCV)

A FRIEND WHO
SEES AS JESUS DOES

If it's mostly sadness that we feel,
There's no way for us to heal
From our memories of the past;
We must find a way to laugh.

Surely, there was something good,
Someone who cared and understood,
A teacher, sibling, friend, or aunt—
Someone who spoke on our behalf;

Someone who saw with Jesus' eyes
Did *not* believe "I'm okay" lies;
Someone who loved with Jesus' heart
And brought light into our "dark".

Then Abraham breathed his last and died at a good old age, an old man and full of years; and he was gathered to his people.

—Genesis 25:8 (NIV)

BEING THERE

Trying to die
Clinging to life

A head nodding yes
Questioning eyes

A few inches gained
A few inches lost

Lungs collapsing
Heart not giving up

Medicine refused
Oxygen accepted

Hands flop
Then arms reach out

Remembering her lover
Gone on ahead

A sister calls
An angel beckons

A nurse gives a pill
A friend, a shampoo

A pastor prays
Lips mouth, "Thank you"

Pain endured
Graciousness displayed.

I silently watch
Holding back tears

Then, on my computer,
Inadequately describe

A humbling portrait
Of courage and faith

May the God who gives endurance and encouragement give you the same attitude of mind toward each other that Christ Jesus had, so that with one mind and one voice you may glorify the God and Father of our Lord Jesus Christ.

—Romans 15:5-6 (NIV)

SOMETIMES HE
SENT ANOTHER

When there's anger in my heart,
And I'm tempted to lash out at my Creator
I remember this—

How in times of past depression
Confusion and deep pain
Jesus stayed with me.

Sometimes he sent another
To listen and cry with me;

In the darkness of my mind,
They lovingly sustained me—

Kept me from self-destruction,
Brought calmness to my spirit,

Delivered me from fear;
I felt his presence in their silence.

When there's anger in my heart,
And I'm tempted to lash out at my Creator
I remember this—

How in times of past depression
Confusion and deep pain
Jesus stayed with me.

Sometimes he sent another
Who could see with eyes like his

Who simply sat and listened
Without interruption—

Not hastening to give answers,
To my bruised and bleeding heart.

In that gift of silence,
I felt deep acceptance.

Sometimes, he sent another and
My heart began to heal.

Accepted

The eye can never say to the hand, "I don't need you."
The head can't say to the feet, "I don't need you."

—1 Corinthians 12:21

ACCEPTING SUPPORT

When I'm stuck in a rut of resentment,
How do I get back to trust, and contentment?

I have a little talk with myself.
I ask Our Father for His help.

I call some friends and ask them to pray.
I take positive action, without delay.

In this way, I show respect for myself
And enjoy mental and emotional health.

I may be a victim but I have a choice;
I can accept my lot or make use of my voice.

I can call for support. Refuse to remain
A captive to any human's chain.

I can prove who I am by doing good.
I don't need to be hostile or start a feud.

Our Father in heaven sees the unjust.
He fights for victims of prejudice.

Praise be to the God and Father of our Lord Jesus Christ. God is the Father who is full of mercy and all comfort. He comforts us every time we have trouble, so when others have trouble, we can comfort them with the same comfort God gives us.

—2 Corinthians 1:3-5 (NCV)

UNDERSTANDING

Sorrow is not my home
Although it often felt like it was.
I'm familiar with tears—
As a child, I bonded with pain.

My heart often returns to that place.
Less frequently, it remains there.
Accepting the hand of mercy and grace,
More quickly I get out of bed.

Although my body is slower,
My mind and spirit persist.
They insist that I, a child of the King,
Step into freedom and joy.

The invitation comes from a friend—
Someone I can trust,
Someone who, with Jesus's eyes,
Sees the pain that still is hidden;

When I finally name it,
Let go of the shame,
And release those who gave it—
Including myself,
That pain no longer grips me.
I am free from it.

My sorrow turns into a rose
I give it others.
My tears mingle with theirs.
Healing flows.

Hope

The Spirit of God, who raised Jesus from the dead, lives in you. And just as God raised Christ Jesus from the dead, he will give life to your mortal bodies by this same Spirit living within you.

—Romans 8:11

GOD'S PROMISE OF STRENGTH

God will strengthen my mortal body;
That's the word I heard him say.

God will strengthen my mortal body;
That's the one I possess, today.

God will strengthen my mortal body.
It may be old, but it's not decayed.

God will strengthen my mortal body,
If from wisdom, I don't stray.

God will strengthen my mortal body.
I will trust him and obey.

God will strengthen my mortal body;
That's the promise he made to me.

God will strengthen my mortal body
And raise it up on resurrection day.

Tell all the nations, "The Lord reigns!" The world stands firm and cannot be shaken. He will judge all peoples fairly.

—Psalm 96:10

GOD IS IN CONTROL

Rulers rise, rulers fall;
God's in charge of it all.

He is merciful and just.
In his wisdom, we can trust.

As we walk in his ways
And offer him our praise,

He breaks every shackle of our heart.
Agents of evil depart.

When we walk in the ways of the Lord,
His *presence* is our reward!

After that, we who are still alive and are left will be caught up together with them in the clouds to meet the Lord in the air. And so we will be with the Lord forever.

—1 Thessalonians 5:17 (NIV)

WITH JESUS
FOR ETERNITY

This world is filled with pain and tears
All will change when Christ appears

Those who live, now, 'neath Jesus reign
Are filled with joy, despite their pain

His gentle Spirit calms their fear
As they advance his kingdom here

How blessed are those who live this truth
And have embraced it from their youth

Though they may have no earthly fame
God hears their prayer "in Jesus' name"

And blesses them in countless ways
For which they always give him praise

When their work on earth is complete
He calls them home. At last they meet

The *One* they were created for
That's all they want, nothing more

There's nothing greater than to be
With Jesus for eternity

Now faith is confidence in what we hope for and assurance about what we do not see.

—Hebrews 11:1 (NIV)

I DON'T LOSE HOPE

He is here when I can't see him
Here when I can't feel him
Here when I can't hear him
Jesus is here.

When I'm not sleeping
When my body's aching
When I have no words to pray
Jesus is here.

When the wind is blowing
When the rain is falling
When I see no rainbow
Jesus is here.

When the night is long
When my friends have gone
When I have no song
Jesus is here.

In these times when faith is tested,
I remember his promises
I recall his faithfulness
I review the times he answered prayer

In this way, my roots grow deeper
Although the path is steeper
I do not turn back in fear
Up ahead, I know I'll see his face

In these times, when faith is tested, I
Get up and read some Scripture
Write down the truth I find there
In response, compose a prayer

In this way, my faith grows stronger
Although the night is longer
I don't give up. Don't lose hope
Up ahead, I know I'll see his face

He is here when I can't see him
Here when I can't feel him
Here when I can't hear him
Jesus is here.

Jesus is here

And we know that God causes everything to work together for the good of those who love God and are called according to his purpose for them. For God knew his people in advance, and he chose them to become like his Son, so that his Son would be the firstborn among many brothers and sisters.

—Romans 8:28-29

GOD PLANNED IN ADVANCE

Jesus,
You knew where I'd be on this day in which
I can't make sense of things.

My mind is foggy.
My body feels weary
Before you created me, you looked ahead and saw me here.

Jesus,
You knew where I'd be on this day in which
I've overcommitted myself.

You are neither surprised
Nor dismayed
Before you created me, you looked ahead and saw me here.

Jesus,
You knew where I'd be on this day in which
My faith is being tested.

You knew what you would do
You knew what you would do when I prayed.
You knew I'd find hope, again.
Before you created me, you looked ahead and saw me here.

Even if the mountains are removed
and the hills displaced,
my devotion will not be removed from you,
nor will my covenant of friendship be displaced,"
says the Lord, the one who has compassion on you.

—Isaiah 54:10 (NET)

UNCEASING
FRIENDSHIP

Always, you hear my plea
Always, you come to me

You are my strength
You are my hope.
You've loved me from eternity.

Always, you hear my plea
Always, you come to me

Jesus, I love you
Jesus, I love you
Oh, Jesus, I love you so much

For years, I did not believe
For years, I could not conceive

I was wanted
I was counted
I was one of your sheep

Always, you heard my plea
Always, you cared for me

Jesus, I love you
Jesus, I love you
Oh, Jesus, I love you so much

You opened my eyes. I see!
You opened my ears. I hear!

In each disaster
You bring me laughter
Your friendship is precious to me

Always, you hear my plea
Always, you come to me

Jesus, I love you
Jesus, I love you
Oh, Jesus, I love you so much

Celebration

I will sing to the Lord as long as I live.
  I will praise my God to my last breath!
May all my thoughts be pleasing to him,
  for I rejoice in the Lord.

—Psalm 104:33-34

ENRAPTURED BY YOUR FACE

Lord, when I think of your love for me
My heart is filled with ecstasy.

The pain and trouble of this earth is small,
I know someday I will leave it all.

I'll live with you for eternity,
Enraptured by your face!

I'm a stranger and a pilgrim here,
I know this more with every passing year.

My footsteps falter and my eyes grow dim,
One thing increases, it's my joy in him.

Jesus, you walk with me every day.
I'm dependent on your grace.

Lord, I wish all my friends could see
The things about you that you've shown to me—

You grow the flowers and you rule the sky.
The deer in the hunters trap does not ask why?

The ocean waters have a boundary
Every creature knows its place.

In all the years you have given me
I see your kind hand of sovereignty.

You came to me in my pain and grief
Your compassion shattered my unbelief.

I sing like a joyful canary
Secure in your embrace.

Lord, when I think of your love for me
My heart is filled with ecstasy.

The pain and trouble of this world is small,
I know someday I will leave it all.

I'll sing to you for eternity,
Enraptured by your face!

Ecstasy

"O death, where is your victory?
O death, where is your sting?"

For sin is the sting that results in death, and the law
gives sin its power. But thank God! He gives us victory
over sin and death through our Lord Jesus Christ.

—1 Corinthians 15:55-57

A PSALM OF VICTORY

Another mountain in my life
Another wave of pain
Another opportunity
For Jesus Christ to reign!

His Spirit in me does the work
I listen to His plan
With confidence obey my Lord
And triumph once again.

I triumph over hellish lies
By him who is the Truth.
He gave His precious blood for me
I need no further proof.

I need no farther proof of love
I need no other sign
But knowledge, wisdom, tongues of joy
And healings too are mine.

Another mountain in my life
A surge of fear or doubt
Another opportunity
For faith to cast it out.

By faith in Him who is my Peace
I am strong and bold
Equipped to conquer fortresses
And break down pride's strong hold.

My confidence is in His Grace
Not in my worthiness
His promise, oath, and covenant
Assure me of success.

Oh hallelujah, praise the Lamb
With gratitude I sing.
In every challenge, change, or threat
He's my victorious King.

Victory

But who am I, and who are my people, that we could give anything to you? Everything we have has come from you, and we give you only what you first gave us!

—1 Chronicles 29:14

A PSALM OF ASTONISHMENT

Father-God,
I am grateful your existence is not dependent
Upon my acknowledgment of you;

You are neither a product of man's perception,
Or an opiate created by his disenchantment.

Long before the world existed, you were
And long after its demise you will be.

You are without beginning and without end,
A concept beyond my understanding!

Who am I that you should pay attention to me?
That you should answer my questions?

What work of mine is worthy of recognition?
All I am and all I've done is nothing before you.

In spite of my arrogance and continual failure
You persist in connecting with me.

You demand a face-to-face confrontation
In which I am repeatedly awed by your grace.

I want to know Christ and the power that raised him from the dead. I want to share in his sufferings and become like him in his death. [11] *Then I have hope that I myself will be raised from the dead.*

—Philippians 3:10-11 (NCV)

A PSALM OF GRATITUDE

No word or song can ever convey
The depth of love he's shown to me.
It is my thankful spirit's way
Of praising him who set me free.

I will sing throughout eternity
Of Jesus' love revealed at Calvary.
He is my only Source of righteousness
Glad praises to his name I now confess.

No power of earth or hell can stand
Before his pure and holy throne,
But he extends his loving hand
And with his truth has mercy shown.

Oh glory, glory to the God of Grace
He has shown his love to one of Adam's race.
He's chosen those from every tribe and shore.
Let praises ring to him whom we adore.

No gift or tribute could I bring
That would pay the honor he is due.
Yet I may bow before my king
And worship him who makes anew.

His Spirit works to mold in purity
The new creation he has made of me.
Sing hallelujah, hallelujah to the Lamb
The unblemished son of God has no flaw.

No pain or sorrow could I feel
That by his touch He could not heal.
Yet, still to suffering He calls me
That I may fellowship in death like He—

That I may know his resurrection power
And comprehend His glory in that hour.
This earthen vessel soon shall pass away.
What blessed hope! He protects me for that day.

Hope

God highly exalted him
and gave him the name
that is above every name,
so that at the name of Jesus
every knee will bow
—in heaven and on earth and under the earth—
and every tongue confess
that Jesus Christ is Lord
to the glory of God the Father.

—Philippians 2:9-11 (NET)

YOU ARE FAR,
FAR ABOVE

You are far, far above
You are far, far above
You are far, far above

Holy, holy, holy, holy, holy, holy
Holy, holy, holy, holy, holy, holy

You came down in love
You came down in love
You came down in love

Holy, holy, holy, holy, holy, holy
Holy, holy, holy, holy, holy, holy

To a people unholy,
a people unloving,
a people corrupted,
a people so angry they mocked and killed you

Holy, holy, holy, holy, holy, holy
Holy, holy, holy, holy, holy, holy

I can't image such love
I can't imagine such love
I can't imagine such love

You are far, far above
You are far, far above
You are far, far above

221

Holy, holy, holy, holy, holy, holy
Holy, holy, holy, holy, holy, holy

You came down in love
You came down in love
You came down in love

Holy, holy, holy, holy, holy, holy
Holy, holy, holy, holy, holy, holy

Jesus, I love you, I praise and adore you,
I bow down before you
My heart is weeping, my heart is rejoicing,
my heart is receiving

Your unimaginable love,
Your unimaginable love,
Your unimaginable love

Unimaginable
love

*Get out of here, Satan," Jesus told him. "For the
Scriptures say,*

*'You must worship the Lord your God
and serve only him.'"*

—Matthew 4:10

WORSHIP GOD ALONE

When hate and anger rise against you
Don't think the arm of flesh can save you

Worship God, alone
Worship God, alone
Worship God, alone

All flesh is grass. It will wither
Hope in one who changes never

Worship God, alone
Worship God, alone
Worship God, alone

Speak the truth. Do not waver
Do what's right. Love your neighbor

Worship God, alone
Worship God, alone
Worship God, alone

Repent, confess, and keep on growing
Forgive, forgive, and keep forgiving

Worship God, alone
Worship God, alone
Worship God, alone

Do not quit the race you're running
Be faithful for Our Savior's coming

Worship God, alone
Worship God, alone
Worship God, alone

Worship God, alone
Bow before his throne

Worship God, Alone

But let me tell you something wonderful, a mystery I'll probably never fully understand. We're not all going to die—but we are all going to be changed. You hear a blast to end all blasts from a trumpet, and in the time that you look up and blink your eyes—it's over. On signal from that trumpet from heaven, the dead will be up and out of their graves, beyond the reach of death, never to die again. At the same moment and in the same way, we'll all be changed. In the resurrection scheme of things, this has to happen: everything perishable taken off the shelves and replaced by the imperishable, this mortal replaced by the immortal. Then the saying will come true:

Death swallowed by triumphant Life!
Who got the last word, oh, Death?
Oh, Death, who's afraid of you now?

It was sin that made death so frightening and law-code guilt that gave sin its leverage, its destructive power. But now in a single victorious stroke of Life, all three— sin, guilt, death—are gone, the gift of our Master, Jesus Christ. Thank God!

—1 Corinthians 15: 52-57 (MSG)

I WILL RISE AND SING

Death has lost its sting
I will rise and sing

Greater than my loss and sorrow
Is God's promise of tomorrow
I will rise
I will rise
I will rise and sing

Death has lost its sting
I will rise and sing

Like a cloud God's love surrounds me
Nothing in this world can harm me
I will rise
I will rise
I will rise and sing

Death has lost its sting
I will rise and sing

With the saints of all the ages
Purchased by the blood of Jesus
I will rise
I will rise
I will rise and sing

Death has lost its sting
I will rise and sing

In this time of pain and trouble
When I doubt and when I struggle
I will rise
I will rise
I will rise and sing

Death has lost its sting
I will rise and sing

I will rise
I will rise
I will rise and sing

ACKNOWLEDGEMENTS

I am grateful for the many people who prayed for me and encouraged me in writing this book. To these four I'm particularly grateful.

My husband John, who did more of his share of household tasks, patiently listened to my many revisions, cheered me when I felt discouraged, and prayed for me

My daughter, Carrie Marks, who carved time out of her teaching schedule at Sacramento City College to read and edit my material

My writing coach Renee Fisher, who urged me to pursue my dream, prayed for me, gave me needed instruction and advice, and cheered me on with enthusiasm

My designer Nelly Murariu, who forgave my lack of knowledge and errors, extended grace, and made my manuscript beautiful.

ABOUT THE AUTHOR

A poet, counselor, and author, Jane Ault writes poems, songs, and books which encourage people grow toward emotional and spiritual maturity—to become more like Jesus.

She's an artistic woman of Scandinavian descent who loves Scripture and meditation, enjoys walks on the lakeshore, and delights in sharing her inspirations with friends over a cup of coffee. Her other creative interests are photography, painting, and card-making.

In partnership with her husband-pastor, she's mentored and counseled people for fifty-one years, gradually developing her gift and love for writing.

They've been married fifty-three years and have two daughters and six grandchildren.

Her previous books are *Emotional Freedom: The Choices We Must Make,* and *Heart Connections: Finding Joy through Openness with God.*

www.ingramcontent.com/pod-product-compliance
Lightning Source LLC
Chambersburg PA
CBHW050112280326
41933CB00010B/1067